FAMILY VOICES

A monologue from
OTHER PLACES

by Harold Pinter

SAMUEL FRENCH

samuelfrench.co.uk

ISBN 978-0-573-12067-1

www.samuelfrench.co.uk
www.samuelfrench.com

FOR AMATEUR PRODUCTION ENQUIRIES

UNITED KINGDOM AND WORLD
EXCLUDING NORTH AMERICA
plays@samuelfrench.co.uk
020 7255 4302/01

Each title is subject to availability from Samuel French, depending upon country of performance.

Other plays by HAROLD PINTER
published and licensed by Samuel French

Celebration

The Birthday Party

The Caretaker

The Collection

The Dumb Waiter

The Homecoming

A Kind of Alaska (from the collection *Other Places*)

The Lover

Mixed Doubles

Mountain Language

A Night Out

One for the Road (from the collection *Other Places*)

One to Another

The Room

A Slight Ache

Victoria Station (from the collection *Other Places*)

Other plays by HAROLD PINTER
licensed by Samuel French

Apart from That

Ashes to Ashes

The Basement

Betrayal

The Black and White

The Dwarfs

The Hothouse

Landscape

Last To Go

Monologue

Moonlight

The New World Order

Night School

No Man's Land

Old Times

Party Time

Precisely

Press Conference

Request Stop

Silence

Tess

That's All

That's Your Trouble

Trouble in the Works

ABOUT THE AUTHOR

Harold Pinter was born in London in 1930. He lived with Antonia Fraser from 1975 until his death on Christmas Eve 2008. (They were married in 1980).

After studying at the Royal Academy of Dramatic Art and the Central School of Speech and Drama, he worked as an actor under the stage name David Baron. Following his success as a playwright, he continued to act under his own name, on stage and screen. He last acted in 2006 when he appeared in Beckett's *Krapp's Last Tape* at the Royal Court Theatre, directed by Ian Rickson.

He wrote twenty-nine plays including *The Birthday Party*, *The Dumb Waiter*, *A Slight Ache*, *The Hothouse*, *The Caretaker*, *The Collection*, *The Lover*, *The Homecoming*, *Old Times*, *No Man's Land*, *Betrayal*, *A Kind of Alaska*, *One For The Road*, *The New World Order*, *Moonlight* and *Ashes to Ashes*. Sketches include *The Black and White*, *Request Stop*, *That's your Trouble*, *Night*, *Precisely*, *Apart From that* and the recently rediscovered, *Umbrellas*.

He directed twenty-seven theatre productions, including James Joyce's *Exiles*, David Mamet's *Oleanna*, seven plays by Simon Gray (one of which was *Butley* in 1971 which he directed the film of three years later) and many of his own plays including his last, *Celebration*, paired with his first, *The Room* at The Almeida Theatre, London in the spring of 2000.

He wrote twenty-one screenplays including *The Pumpkin Eater*, *The Servant*, *The Go-Between*, *The French Lieutenant's Woman* and *Sleuth*.

In 2005 he received the Nobel Prize for Literature. Other awards include the Companion of Honour for services to Literature, the Legion D'Honneur, the European Theatre Prize the Laurence Olivier Award and the Moliere D'Honneur for lifetime achievement. In 1999 he was made a Companion of Literature by the Royal Society of Literature. Harold Pinter was awarded eighteen honorary degrees.

CHARACTERS

VOICE 1, a young man
VOICE 2, a woman
VOICE 3, a man

FAMILY VOICES

First broadcast on BBC Radio 3 on 22nd January, 1981, with the following cast:

VOICE 1	Michael Kitchen
VOICE 2	Peggy Ashcroft
VOICE 3	Mark Dignam

Directed by Peter Hall

First presented on the stage in a "platform performance" by the National Theatre, London, on 13th February, 1981, with the same cast and director. The décor was by John Bury.

It was subsequently presented as part of the triple bill *Other Places** in the Cottesloe auditorium of the National Theatre, London, on 14th October, 1982, with the following cast:

VOICE 1	Nigel Havers
VOICE 2	Anna Massey
VOICE 3	Paul Rogers

Directed by Peter Hall
Designed by John Bury

* *A Kind of Alaska, One for the Road* and *Victoria Station* are available separately in Acting Editions published by Samuel French.

To Mick Goldstein

VOICE 1 I am having a very nice time.

The weather is up and down, but surprisingly warm, on the whole, more often than not.

I hope you're feeling well, and not as peaky as you did, the last time I saw you.

No, you didn't feel peaky, you felt perfectly well, you simply looked peaky.

Do you miss me?

I am having a very nice time and I hope you are glad of that.

At the moment I am dead drunk.

I had five pints in *The Fishmongers Arms* tonight, followed by three double scotches, and literally rolled home.

When I say home I can assure you that my room is extremely pleasant. So is the bathroom. Extremely pleasant. I have some very pleasant baths indeed in the bathroom. So does everybody else in the house. They all lie quite naked in the bath and have very pleasant baths indeed. All the people in the house go about saying what a superb bath and bathroom the one we share is, they go about telling literally everyone they meet what lovely baths you can get in this place, more or less unparalleled, to put it bluntly.

It's got a lot to do with the landlady, who is a Mrs Withers, a person who turns out to be an utterly charming person, of impeccable credentials.

When I said I was drunk I was of course making a joke.

I bet you laughed.

Mother?

Did you get the joke? You know I never touch alcohol.

I like being in this enormous city, all by myself. I expect to make friends in the not too distant future.

I expect to make girlfriends too.

I expect to meet a very nice girl. Having met her, I shall bring her home to meet my mother.

I like walking in this enormous city, all by myself. It's fun to know no one at all. When I pass people in the street they don't realize that I don't know them from Adam. They know other people and even more other people know them, so they naturally think that even if I don't know them I know the other people. So they look at me, they try to catch my eye, they expect me to speak. But as I do not know them I do not speak. Nor do I ever feel the slightest temptation to do so.

You see, Mother, I am not lonely, because all that has ever happened to me is with me, keeps me company; my childhood, for example, through which you, my mother, and he, my father, guided me.

I get on very well with my landlady, Mrs Withers. She tells me I am her solace. I have a drink with her at lunchtime and another one at teatime and then take her for a couple in the evening at *The Fishmongers Arms*.

She was in the Women's Air Force in the Second World War. Don't drop a bollock, Charlie, she's fond of saying, Call him Flight Sergeant and he'll be happy as a pig in shit.

You'd really like her, Mother.

I think it's dawn. I can see it coming up. Another day. A day I warmly welcome. And so I shall end this letter to you, my dear mother, with my love.

VOICE 2 Darling. Where are you? The flowers are wonderful here. The blooms. You so loved them. Why do you never write?

I think of you and wonder how you are. Do you ever think of me? Your mother? Ever? At all?

Have you changed your address?

Have you made friends with anyone? A nice boy? Or a nice girl?

There are so many nice boys and nice girls about. But please don't get mixed up with the other sort. They can land you in such terrible trouble. And you'd hate it so. You're so scrupulous, so particular.

I often think that I would love to live happily ever after with you and your young wife. And she would be such a lovely wife to you and I would have the occasional dinner with you both. A dinner I would be quite happy to cook myself, should you both be tired after your long day, as I'm sure you will be.

I sometimes walk the cliff path and think of you. I think of the times you walked the cliff path, with your father, with cheese sandwiches. Didn't you? You both sat on the clifftop and ate my cheese sandwiches together. Do you remember our little joke? Munch, munch. We had a damn good walk, your father would say. You mean you had a good munch munch, I would say. And you would both laugh.

Darling. I miss you. I gave birth to you. Where are you?

I wrote to you three months ago, telling you of your father's death. Did you receive my letter?

VOICE 1 I'm not at all sure that I like the people in this house, apart from Mrs Withers and her daughter, Jane. Jane is a schoolgirl who works hard at her homework.

She keeps her nose to the grindstone. This I find impressive. There's not too much of that about these days. But I'm not so sure about the other people in this house.

One is an old man.

The one who is an old man retires early. He is bald.

The other is a woman who wears red dresses.

The other one is another man.

He is big. He is much bigger than the other man. His hair is black. He has black eyebrows and black hair on the back of his hands.

I ask Mrs Withers about them but she will talk of nothing but her days in the Women's Air Force in the Second World War.

I have decided that Jane is not Mrs Withers' daughter but her grand-daughter. Mrs Withers is seventy. Jane is fifteen. That I am convinced is the truth.

At night I hear whispering from the other rooms and do not understand it. I hear steps on the stairs but do not dare go out to investigate.

VOICE 2 As your father grew closer to his death he spoke more and more of you, with tenderness and bewilderment. I consoled him with the idea that you had left home to make him proud of you. I think I succeeded in this. One of his last sentences was: Give him a slap on the back from me. Give him a slap on the back from me.

VOICE 1 I have made a remarkable discovery. The old man who is bald and who retires early is named Withers. Benjamin Withers. Unless it is simply a coincidence it must mean that he is a relation.

I asked Mrs Withers what the truth of this was. She poured herself a gin and looked at it before she drank it. Then she looked at me and said: You are my little pet. I've always wanted a little pet but I've never had one and now I've got one.

Sometimes she gives me a cuddle, as if she were my mother.

But I haven't forgotten that I have a mother and that you are my mother.

VOICE 2 Sometimes I wonder if you remember that you have a mother.

VOICE 1 Something has happened. The woman who wears red dresses stopped me and asked me into her room for a cup of tea. I went into her room. It was far bigger than I had expected, with sofas and curtains and veils and shrouds and rugs and soft material all over the walls, dark blue. Jane was sitting on a sofa doing her homework, by the look of it. I was invited to sit on the same sofa. Tea had already been made and stood ready, in a china teaset, of a most elegant design. I was given a cup. So was Jane, who smiled at me. I haven't introduced myself, the woman said, my name is Lady Withers. Jane sipped her tea with her legs up on the sofa. Her stockinged toes came to rest on my thigh. It wasn't the biggest sofa in the world. Lady Withers sat opposite us on a substantially bigger sofa. Her dress, I decided, wasn't red but pink. Jane was in green, apart from her toes, which were clad in black. Lady Withers asked me about you, Mother. She asked me about my mother. I said, with absolute conviction, that you were the best mother in the world. She asked me to call her Lally. And to call Jane Jane. I said I did call Jane Jane. Jane gave me a bun. I think it was a bun. Lady Withers bit into her bun. Jane bit into her bun, her toes now resting on my lap. Lady Withers seemed to be enjoying her bun, on her sofa. She finished it and picked up another. I had never seen so many buns. One quick glance told me they were perched on cakestands, all over the room. Lady Withers went through her second bun with no trouble at all and was at once on to another. Jane, on the other hand, chewed almost dreamily at her bun and when a currant was left stranded on her upper lip she licked it off, without haste. I could not reconcile this with the fact that her toes were quite restless, even agitated. Her mother, eating, was measured, serene; her toes, not eating, were agitated, highly strung, some would say hysterical. My bun tuned out to be rock solid. I bit into it, it jumped out of my mouth and bounced into my lap. Jane's feet caught it. It calmed her toes down. She juggled the bun, with some expertise, along them. I recalled that, in an early exchange between us, she had told me she wanted to be an acrobat.

VOICE 2 Darling. Where are you? Why do you never write? Nobody knows your whereabouts. Nobody knows if you are alive or dead. Nobody can find you. Have you changed your name?

If you are alive you are a monster. On his deathbed your father cursed you. He cursed me too, to tell the truth. He cursed everyone in sight. Except that you were not in sight. I do not blame you entirely for your father's ill humour, but your absence and silence were a great burden on him, a weariness to him. He died in lamentation and oath. Was that your wish? Now I am alone, apart from Millie, who sometimes comes over from Dover. She is some consolation. Her eyes well with tears when she speaks of you, your dear sister's eyes well with tears. She has made a truly happy marriage and has a lovely little boy. When he is older he will want to know where his uncle is. What shall we say?

Or perhaps you will arrive here in a handsome new car, one day, in the not too distant future, in a nice new suit, quite out of the blue, and hold me in your arms.

VOICE 1 Lady Withers stood up. As Jane is doing her homework, she said, perhaps you would care to leave and come again another day. Jane withdrew her feet, my bun clasped between her big two toes. Yes of course, I said, unless Jane would like me to help her with her homework. No thank you, said Lady Withers, I shall help her with her homework.

What I didn't say is that I am thinking of offering myself out as a tutor. I consider that I would make an excellent tutor, to the young, in any one of a number of subjects. Jane would be an ideal pupil. She possesses a true love of learning. That is the sense of her one takes from her every breath, her every sigh and exhalation. When she turns her eyes upon you you see within her eyes, raw, untutored, unexercised but willing, a deep love of learning.

These are midnight thoughts, Mother, although the time is ten twenty-three, precisely.

VOICE 2 Darling?

VOICE 1 While I was lying in my bath this afternoon, thinking on these things, there was apparently a knock on the front door. The man with black hair apparently opened the door. Two women stood on the doorstep. They said they were my mother and my sister, and asked for me. He denied knowledge of me. No, he had not heard of me. No, there was no one of that name resident. This was a family house, no strangers admitted. No, they got on very well, thank you very much, without intruders. I suggest, he said, that you both go back to where you come from, and stop bothering innocent hardworking people with your slanders and your libels, these all too predictable excrescences of the depraved mind at the end of its tether. I can smell your sort a mile off and I am quite prepared to put you both on a charge of malicious mischief, insulting behaviour and vagabondage, in other words wandering around on doorsteps knowingly, without any visible means of support. So piss off out of it before I call a copper.

I was lying in my bath when the door opened. I thought I had locked it. My name's Riley, he said, How's the bath? Very nice, I said. You've got a wellknit yet slender frame, he said, I thought you only a snip, I never imagined you would be as wellknit and slender as I now see you are. Oh thank you, I said. Don't thank me, he said, It's God you have to thank. Or your mother. I've just dismissed a couple of imposters at the front door. We'll get no more shit from that quarter. He then sat on the edge of the bath and recounted to me what I've just recounted to you.

It interests me that my father wasn't bothered to make the trip.

VOICE 2 I hear your father's step on the stair. I hear his cough. But his step and his cough fade. He does not open the door.

Sometimes I think I have always been sitting like this. I sometimes think I have always been sitting like this, alone by an indifferent fire, curtains closed, night, winter.

You see, I have my thoughts too. Thoughts no one else knows I have, thoughts none of my family ever knew I had. But I write of them to you now, wherever you are.

What I mean is that when, for example, I was washing your hair, with the most delicate shampoo, and rinsing, and then drying your hair so gently with my soft towel, so that no murmur came from you, of discomfort or unease, and then looked into your eyes, and saw you look into mine, knowing that you wanted no one else, no one at all, knowing that you were entirely happy in my arms, I knew also, for example, that I was at the same time sitting by an indifferent fire, alone in winter, in eternal night without you.

VOICE 1 Lady Withers plays the piano. They were sitting, the three women, about the room. About the room were bottles of a vin rosé, of a pink I shall never forget. They sipped their wine from such lovely glass, an elegance of gesture and grace I thought long dead. Lady Withers wore a necklace around her alabaster neck, a neck amazingly young. She played Schumann. She smiled at me. Mrs Withers and Jane smiled at me. I took a seat. I took it and sat in it. I am in it. I will never leave it.

Oh Mother, I have found my home, my family. Little did I ever dream I could know such happiness.

VOICE 2 Perhaps I should forget all about you. Perhaps I should curse you as your father cursed you. Oh I pray, I pray your life is a torment to you. I wait for your letter begging me to come to you. I'll spit on it.

VOICE 1 Mother, Mother, I've had the most unpleasant, the most mystifying encounter, with the man who calls himself Mr Withers. Will you give me your advice?

Come in here, son, he called. Look sharp. Don't mess about. I haven't got all night. I went in. A jug. A basin. A bicycle.

You know where you are? he said. You're in my room. It's not Euston station. Get me? It's a true oasis.

This is the only room in this house where you can pick up a caravanserai to all points West. Compris? Comprende? Get me? Are you prepared to follow me down the mountain? Look at me. My name's Withers. I'm there or thereabouts. Follow? Embargo on all duff terminology. With me? Embargo on all things redundant. All areas in that connection verboten. You're in a disease-ridden land, boxer. Keep your weight on all the left feet you can lay your hands on. Keep dancing. The old foxtrot is the classical response but that's not the response I'm talking about. Nor am I talking about the other response. Up the slaves. Get me? This is a place of creatures, up and down stairs. Creatures of the rhythmic splits, the rhythmic sideswipes, the rums and roulettes, the macaroni tatters, the dumplings in jam mayonnaise, a catapulting ordure of gross and ramshackle shenanigans, open-ended paraphernalia. Follow me? It all adds up. It's before you and behind you. I'm the only saviour of the grace you find yourself wanting in. Mind how you go. Look sharp. Get my drift? Don't let it get too mouldy. Watch the mould. Get the feel of it, sonny, get the density. Look at me.

And I did.

VOICE 2 I am ill.

VOICE 1 It was like looking into a pit of molten lava, Mother. One look was enough for me.

VOICE 2 Come to me.

VOICE 1 I joined Mrs Withers for a Campari and soda in the kitchen. She spoke of her youth. I was a right titbit, she said. I was like a piece of plum duff. They used to come from miles to try their luck. I fell head over heels with a man in the Fleet Air Arm. He adored me. They had him murdered because they didn't want us to know happiness. I could have married him and had tons of sons. But oh no. He went down with his ship. I heard it on the wireless.

VOICE 2 I wait for you.

VOICE 1 Later that night Riley and I shared a cup of cocoa in his quarters. I like slender lads, Riley said. Slender but strong. I've never made any secret of it. But I've had to restrain myself, I've had to keep a tight rein on my inclinations. That's because my deepest disposition is towards religion. I've always been a deeply religious man. You can imagine the tension this creates in my soul. I walk about in a constant state of spiritual, emotional, psychological and physical tension. It's breathtaking, the discipline I'm called upon to exert. My lust is unimaginably violent but it goes against my best interests, which are to keep on the right side of God. I'm a big man, as you see, I could crush a slip of a lad such as you to death, I mean the death that is love, the death I understand love to be. But meet it is that I keep those desires shackled in handcuffs and leg-irons. I'm good at that sort of thing because I'm a policeman by trade. And I'm highly respected. I'm highly respected both in the force and in church. The only place where I'm not highly respected is in this house. They don't give a shit for me here. Although I've always been a close relation. Of a sort. I'm a fine tenor but they never invite me to sing. I might as well be living in the middle of the Sahara desert. There are too many women here, that's the trouble. And it's no use talking to Baldy. He's well away. He lives in another area, best known to himself. I like health and strength and intelligent conversation. That's why I took a fancy to you, chum, apart from the fact that I fancy you. I've got no one to talk to. These women treat me like a leper. Even though I am a relation. Of a sort.

What relation?

Is Lady Withers Jane's mother or sister?

If either is the case why isn't Jane called Lady Jane Withers? Or perhaps she is. Or perhaps neither is the case? Or perhaps Mrs Withers is actually the Honourable Mrs Withers? But if that is the case what does that make Mr Withers? And which Withers is he anyway? I mean what relation is he to the rest of the Witherses? And who is Riley?

But if you find me bewildered, anxious, confused, uncertain and afraid, you also find me content. My life possesses shape. The house has a very warm atmosphere, as you have no doubt gleaned. And as you have no doubt noted from my account I talk freely to all its inhabitants, with the exception of Mr Withers, to whom no one talks, to whom no one refers, with evidently good reason. But I rarely leave the house. No one seems to leave the house. Riley leaves the house but rarely. He must be a secret policeman. Jane continues to do a great deal of homework while not apparently attending any school. Lady Withers never leaves the house. She has guests. She receives guests. Those are the steps I hear on the stairs at night.

VOICE 3 I know your mother has written to you to tell you that I am dead. I am not dead. I am very far from being dead, although lots of people have wished me dead, from time immemorial, you especially. It is you who have prayed for my death, from time immemorial. I have heard your prayers. They ring in my ears. Prayers yearning for my death. But I am not dead.

Well, that is not entirely true, not entirely the case. I'm lying. I'm leading you up the garden path, I'm playing about, I'm having my bit of fun, that's what. Because I am dead. As dead as a doornail. I'm writing to you from my grave. A quick word for old time's sake. Just to keep in touch. An old hullo out of the dark. A last kiss from Dad.

I'll probably call it a day after this canter. Not much more to say. All a bit of a sweat. Why am I taking the trouble? Because of you, I suppose, because you were such a loving son. I'm smiling, as I lie in this glassy grave.

Do you know why I use the word glassy? Because I can see out of it.

Lots of love, son. Keep up the good work.

There's only one thing bothers me, to be quite frank. While there is, generally, absolute silence everywhere, absolute silence throughout all the hours, I still hear, occasionally, a dog barking. I hear this dog. Oh, it frightens me.

VOICE 1 They have decided on a name for me. They call me Bobo. Good-morning, Bobo, they say, or, See you in the morning, Bobo, or, Don't drop a goolie, Bobo, or, Don't forget the diver, Bobo, or, Keep your eye on the ball, Bobo, or, Keep this side of the tramlines, Bobo, or, How's the lead in your pencil, Bobo, or, How's tricks in the sticks, Bobo, or, Don't get too much gum in your gumboots, Bobo.

The only person who does not call me Bobo is the old man. He calls me nothing. I call him nothing. I don't see him. He keeps to his room. I don't go near it. He is old and will die soon.

VOICE 2 The police are looking for you. You may remember that you are still under twenty-one. They have issued your precise description to all the organs. They will not rest, they assure me, until you are found. I have stated my belief that you are in the hands of underworld figures who are using you as a male prostitute. I have declared in my affidavit that you have never possessed any strength of character whatsoever and that you are palpably susceptible to even the most blatant form of flattery and blandishment. Women were your downfall, even as a nipper. I haven't forgotten Françoise the French maid or the woman who masqueraded under the title of governess, the infamous Miss Carmichael. You will be found, my boy, and no mercy will be shown to you.

VOICE 1 I'm coming back to you, Mother, to hold you in my arms. I am coming home.

I am coming also to clasp my father's shoulder. Where is the old boy? I'm longing to have a word with him. Where is he? I've looked in all the usual places, including the old summerhouse, but I can't find him. Don't tell me he's left home at his age? That would be inexpressibly skittish a gesture, on his part. What have you done with him, Mother?

VOICE 2 I'll tell you what, my darling. I've given you up as a very bad job. Tell me one last thing. Do you think the word love means anything?

VOICE 1 I am on my way back to you. I am about to make the journey back to you. What will you say to me?

VOICE 3 I have so much to say to you. But I am quite dead. What I have to say to you will never be said.

Curtain.

FURNITURE AND PROPERTY LIST

Onstage: 3 chairs

Offstage: Nil

LIGHTING PLOT

Property fittings required: nil

To open: Lighting up on **Voice 1**

Cue 1	**Voice 1**: "...with my love." *Lighting up on* **Voice 2**	(Page 2)
Cue 2	**Voice 1**: "...on the stairs at night." *Lighting up on* **Voice 3**	(Page 11)
Cue 3	**Voice 3**: "...will never be said." *Blackout*	(Page 13)

EFFECTS PLOT

No cues

www.ingramcontent.com/pod-product-compliance
Lightning Source LLC
Chambersburg PA
CBHW070455050426
42450CB00012B/3293